a monk at sunset

john l. ng
lent 2018

cover image
"monk at rest," an original brush painting by the author

ekklesia ministries, new york
monkatsunset@yahoo.com
ISBN 978-1-387-64358-5

about the title and these unfinished thoughts

there is a weariness that sleep cannot refresh. that weariness comes not from physical fatigue, but from an estrangement of souls and animus of spirits with others. during these latter years, i walked away from professional ministries and retreated to a solace of solitude. some time later, i offered a friend a rationale for this self-imposed solace. my friend smirked incredulously. his skepticism has merits. being human as we are, it is impossible to live without others. this lonesome existentialism would be more lonely. God made us for and with others.

yet i confess that without solitude, "phatic" noises are all i have when with others. cognitive, and emotive, thoughts that stir within my soul remain a smoldering smog without the cleansing air of solitude. it is a chosen quietude that trains me in self recovery and self discovery. the church fathers and mothers agree that perhaps the highest form of spirituality is a self-awareness. knowing God in Christ profoundly is knowing self deeply; knowing self profoundly precedes knowing God in Christ deeply. that ontological awareness is unfolding daily. my meditative proclivity trains this weary soul to cut a clearer path toward spending time and space (the meaning of contemplation) with God, and with others.

monk at sunset - "monk" is from μοναχος that means solitary. and i am sixty-something and live on sunset view.

"Now is the winter of our discontent..."
Shakespeare's *Richard III*

my faith pilgrimage is an outward journey that has turned inward. in the Season of Pentecost of 2011, i walked away from my professional ministries as seminary professor and church pastor and retreated to my solace at sunset. it was a decision not unexpected. between the seminary's institutional impiety and the institutional church's ineptitude, any residue of energetic drive to continue had dissipated. i was simply spent.

then during the Season of Pentecost of 2013, i also retreated from community to seek solitude at sunset. my second walk away did not mean that i did not find meaning in community. our shared human pathology was simply too much for this weak soul. it was increasingly, excruciatingly difficult to practice life together with people. it would take a saint to dwell among people. i am not that person.

"It is not through virtue that I live in solitude, but through weakness, those who live in the midst of men are the strong ones." this admission by Abba Matoes, an early church desert hermit, gave me courage as well as credence to retreat from community. it is a confession of emotive weakness and a kind of spiritual laziness to engage in social intercourse. the fabric of my spirituality is simply too flimsy to portage the heaviness of human relationships. at the sunset of my years, my soul is tattered from being with people.

i seek solitude not because i no longer believe in community, nor because i think i am more spiritual than others. i seek solitude simply due to my weakness of heart, soul, body and mind. living with people has become a grievous endeavor. i fail others and others fail me. we are only being human. strangely, in long moments of solace, i still long for community. for years i have maintained that being human that we are, we would be destitute without other humans in community. it is self-evident that our Creator has made us for community. without it we would be incomplete, inadequate and unfinished. so in earnest, during my middle years, i sought meaningful relationships. in time, these relationships became a community of friendships.

why do two people become friends? why some people never become friends? who knows! the human heart is dark with mystery. who can explain why my friends and I become friends. why some never become close; why some abandon what we have; why some don't invest in what we can have. it is also a mystery why i choose one to be friend but not with another. two men seem to share similar disposition – they are intelligent, articulate, successful and arrogant. one becomes a close friend, the other remains a distant acquaintance.

like all living things, friendship seems to have a life cycle. there is a beginning, an end and an enduring middle. one friendship has last four decades; another barely survived four years. sometimes i wonder how futile are our efforts to build friendships. it seems no matter what we do or fail to do, a friendship has its own life. it rises and ebbs; it crawls under shadows and runs through sunlight. just as inexplicably when two people become friends, so it is when two people stop being friends.

another may never have thought of me as a close friend and betrayed me for a more nobler cause. two never got close - one simply did not have the right stuff to be close to another human being; the other did not have the generosity of stuff to spend on a friendship. so we remain friends but at a social distance. one day another walked away without a word. another wanted more from what i could give. it is plainly costly of soul, spirit and body to share bread with companions. i wish i could simply sit back and enjoy what i have. but i have not.

Cicero, the great Roman orator and thinker, is convinced that without a shared nobility a truer friendship is impossible. He writes: a good friendship is a great accomplishment that requires no small endeavor. one ought to seek it within all human attainment. but friendship can only be nurtured between two noble persons who possess a certain character of integrity, equity and kindness.

St Paul seems to hint at the same nobility: *finally, brothers and sisters, whatever is true* (transparency, forthrightness, my rendition), *whatever is honorable* (upstanding, dignified), *whatever is just* (equitable, filial duty), *whatever is pure* (single-minded, wholesome), *whatever is lovely* (graceful, winsome), *whatever is commendable* (admirable, respectful), *if there is any excellence* (superlative, virtuous), *if there is anything worthy of praise* (gratuitous, laudable), *contemplate on these things.* (Philippians 4.8 - 9)

a friend once demurred that i had treated strangers more considerately than with her. another quipped that he had treated me more selflessly than with others. and another lamented that to spend any time with me was a difficult chore. realistically, in their own words were they not addressing the necessity of noble behavior in friendships. without the above noble virtues, can a friendship endure or even be nurtured. life's journeys are difficult enough without the burdens of friendship. in those many murky moments, friendships are impossible simply because of this priori of nobility. i realize all the more that an enduring friendship can only be between two honorable individuals. in the winter of my discontent, the warmth of fewer friendships is waning for their noble laxity.

then there is my domestic community. these familial relationships have an enduring love. and we enter this love viscerally. we simply love one another; the love code is in our blood. but we love one another in our own way that are more uneven than mutual. there is my marriage. it is simply amazing how my wife and i have shared a bed, a financial account, a family and a called pastoral work, but not a compatibility of perception and understanding of the world in which we live and have our being. some time ago, in a moment of profound transparency, and weakness, i confessed to a group of strangers that after forty years of marriage, i realized that our relationship is predicated by an irreversible misunderstanding.

in this pervasive misunderstanding, we differ in the ways we listen, acquire knowledge, integrate information, understand words. we differ in the methods we express thoughts, articulate convictions, practice values and beliefs. at sunset, i have accepted that no amount of efforts by us can dissipate this fog of misunderstanding. there are many moments when we simply do not like each other. and yet we are irrevocably in love with each other. both in our separate ways have decided to stick to what we are undeniably stuck with. when we stand before God, in the presence of the congregation, even in our emotional longing, both of us simply know that through the years we would be mutually committed and would grow old together.

---

* *in ancient Hebrew culture, the numerical 40 in time represents a longevity. similar to the Chinese 10,000 that means an immeasurably high number.*

then there is my immediate and extended families. if there are people in this global village whom i love with both mind and heart, it would be this family that includes my children and grandchildren, my sister and my wife's siblings. whenever we gather as family, it is a wonder-full feeling to embrace that irresistible assurance that my family has a future with God. in God's grace, our family's legacy of faith will continue from this generation into the next. as fathers and mothers, as aunts and uncles, as brothers and sisters, we communally look to God to cultivate an amorous space we all call home.

but love cannot be impervious to all that is going on in an imperfect community. every time we gather as family, there is another feeling, a haunting feeling of ineptitude. i take a private sigh reassured that God will complete what He has begun. i also know that there is little i can do to make God love my family any more or any less. whether self-imposed or by default, the task of family building falls on me. being its elder, my priestly and pastoral tasks are always before me. at every gathering, i have the awesome, and awful, task of providing a theistic content and context for my family. be it in celebration or in mourning, the task fell on me to interpret the presence of God into the contemplation of my family.

none of this is easy nor should be taken lightly. at all times, i do not feel up to the task. my soul whines bitterly in private for what is expected of me. waiting upon God to do his work of grace and waiting upon my family to pay attention requires enormous amount of long suffering. it is plainly nerve wrecking each time i enter that family gathering. too much is required and too much is taken out of me. after they leave, my anxious devotion for their well being lingers with me.

there is a remote corner in our familial community, where a few extended family members loiter. they keep to themselves; they don't sit in the living room. whether they are unpleasant or uncomfortable, they neither give nor receive from what we do and say. as we seek to build family, they remain innocuously quiet. it is hard work to love them; it is harder work to like them. i often wonder where would they be to find themselves when they are not with family.

then there is my third community, a gathering of congregants of several churches. each time i enter this community, i wrestle with doubts and dreads. mainly because i have never found a sense of community here. however one defines community, i never found it at church. in "Life Together," Bonheoffer offers that we do not have the prerogative to choose nor change our fellowship. it is what it is and it isn't what it isn't. when we enter it, we must find a sense of belonging and endeavor to participate its life and work.

through the years, as pastor and as congregant, i have sought to practice hospitality. but mostly we have remained intimate strangers. we share the same sanctuary, we sing the same tunes, we eat the same food, we share the same work, but we have nothing else the same. we do not adhere to the same worldview. our meanings are different, even contradictory. at all times, there is a social distance for lack of transparency. we simply do not know one another well enough to feel comfortable when we have life together.

toward the end, i realize acutely that for forty years and more i practice a false presence in the church. psychology calls it impression management. as manager of others' impression of me, i play the role, i act the part, i say the right phrasings, the right intonation, the right cadence. i dress for the occasions. in truth, i have always doubted that those under my pastoral care or those who share a mutual care would not like the real me. underneath the many guises i never feel the freedom to be myself.

there are two reasons why at sunset i have retreated from church community. the first is simply our share human pathology. my fellow congregants, including me, could not relinquish what i have longed for. years ago, a congregant, who has since become a good friend, beheld me at church and confessed that he had never known a pastor personally. in a private moment, i also confessed that if he cut me with a knife i would bleed just like him. what sealed our friendship during those earlier years was his realization that just like him i was very human. being human that i was, my neediness needed attending. when i enter the church, intuitively i seek four common graces: loyalty, conversations, sensibility and quietude.

loyalty in relationships is a virtue that rises above our imperfection. it is personal commitment; it is a sense of unconditional acceptance; it is mutuality. just as i pledge allegiance to stick by the people i am with, i also expect others to reciprocate. i confess that i seldom find loyalty in church. there is a long trek of betrayals, from those whom i lead and serve together. when my leadership is assaulted, few in my team come to my defense. when my integrity is questioned, few vouch for me. when my soul is in pain, few seem to care.

for community to share a commonality, meaningful conversation is that fresh air that brings clarity to the murkiness of disagreements and misunderstanding. it seems few of us know how to express our thoughts. worst, almost none of us knows how to listen for thoughts. being human that we all are, clumsy communication is normal. seldom do i find meaningful conversation with my fellow congregants. when we talk, either we shout over one another or commit thoughtless chatter.

social sensibility is that common courtesy we extend to one another. St Paul's grace-full words cause me to crave for this grace even more: *so if there is any encouragement in*

Christ, any comfort from love, any participation in the Spirit, any affection and sympathy, complete my joy by being of the same mind (mind of Christ), having the same love (love of Christ), . . . do nothing from rivalry or conceit, . . . let each of you look not only to his own interests, but also to the interests of others. we simply are not able or willing to consider others' interests first. many congregants are good people. but they are not nice. there is little etiquette in God's church.

quietude of disposition is a kind of serenity that prevails a congregational meeting, a church board meeting, a fellowship meeting. the level of phatic noises is deafening. when we are at prayer, there is that hum of senseless music in the background. when an issue is at hand, there is that senseless talking without quiet listening. when i enter the church, there seems always a din of dissonance. what i long for is a quietude in contemplation - a sharing of space with God and with one another.

for all these years, the discord of community from its lack of these graces robs me of confidence in community. in confessed shame, and guilt, i share Abba Matoes's confession of weakness when coping with the ungraceful frays of community. i have not rejected the church community. how can i - to completely retreat for church is self-contradictory. i still go to church on the Lord's day; i still participate in life group fellowship; i still invite others to my home for food and fellowship. community is still a necessity in every human person. the only change at sunset is that i seek solace of solitude more eagerly. being in community has drained much charismatic [†] energy out of me. i just don't have the zealous drive to be or do pastoral work in community.

[†] *its etymology comes from the Greek* χαϱις, *from which we get grace, gracefulness, gracious, giftedness, joyfulness, charisma, and here charismatic.*

the second reason why i have retreated from community is simply my astonishment that the power that i long for is not the empowerment i embody for pastoral work. Rodney Clapp, an American writer in another matter, writes that: much of our difficulty in being Christians is due to awkwardness, a deficiency of skill in deploying our heartfelt dispositions. . . a lack of gracefulness." at sunset, i retreat to solitude in earnest because this overwhelming sense of not-up-to-it-ness is ubiquitous in all communal endeavors.

there are many affirming moments of incredible euphoria in church. the euphoric rush during my creative preparation and task performance has no rival. and yet, in the remains of my day, when everything is said and done, these grace-full moments cannot usurp the overwhelming feelings that i did not do it well. i realize that my soft soul is discouraged of purpose, weary of duty, and tiresomeness of well meaning in a world of hard corners.

some time ago, a successful businessman reached out to me after he had turned the page from making money to making church work his profit. between bites at a Cheesecake Factory he wondered out loud if he could translate his business success into ministry success. he asked me multiple questions but then preceded to answer them himself. finally i interrupted his soliloquy with a cynical smile, "you know, you're a smart guy. i'm sure you will figure it out." when we parted company, he turned and shouted, "can i call you from time to time. you're expert in these things." i offered another cynical smile, "of course. any time. but sooner or later, you will discover that i know nothing, and what i know is worthless."

> *"You were the only one who understood me.*
> *And you got it wrong."*
> Georg Wilhelm Friedrich Hegel, the German philosopher, to his
> best and favorite student

old age creeps in a deeper sense of loneliness and
sadness. i have always been a sad loner. but it was
never like this. this slow nagging realization that i have
never been understood by others and that there is a
pervasive misunderstanding with others weights
heavy. once upon a time i wanted to believe that if the
people i care for and work with can make
conversations, in time we would share a common
language toward mutual understanding.

some time ago, in a moment of existential weakness, it
seeped out that is a profound misunderstand in my
marriage. something we will never overcome. this
pervasive misunderstanding is not exclusive in my
marriage. it hangs over all my relationships. so much
of our pathology contributes to it. we were raised
wrong. we were never taught to listen. along the way
our personality has evolved into a pathos of fears,
biases and prejudices. our experiences have shaped
our unrealistic, subconscious assumptions and
expectations.

we all have learned the eccentric word meanings no
other shares. and we have but a narrow repertoire of
vernaculars to express our unformed thoughts. adding
to that deficiency there is our limited knowledge of all
things pertinent. and the timing of our conversations is
never quite timely to the one we are speaking. on

memories are faulty – we remember things not as they were but as we remember them. what people hear is seldom what we say; what we say seldom is what we mean; what we mean is seldom understood by the other.

human communication at best is clumsy, and at worst, it is disinformation. the irony is that the closer we are with someone, the more difficult it is to make conversation. with all the variables listed above, there is the ubiquity of past grudges, disappointments and hard feelings. they get in the way of every present exchanges. our ear tunnels are clogged with these residual memories. any new sound has to travel through that sewage. by the time it gets to our cognition, its original intent is already contaminated.

just the other day, a misunderstand between a friend and i silenced our communication. separately we both prayed in earnest for the other. finally one of us made up an excuse to reach out to the other. as we cautiously talked, i realized that it was an misunderstand. many years of mindless selfishness and unintentional insensibility had piled a heap of unspoken grudges.

unbeknown to each other, while one was trying to be transparent, the other was seeking to hide from honesty. when one was going through something, the other was oblivious. while one was growing in one direction, the other was developing another formation. during the last communication, a misunderstand was already percolating. as earnest as we tried to clear the air, when we left the other, both realized privately that the air was not cleared. i did not know where my friend went after we parted company, but i retreated to solitude at sunset.

quaestio mihi factus sum
i am become a question to myself
Augustine

solace of solitude at sunset is a good place; it is a better place than community. i still believe that we were created for others. to journey alone on this barren land would be lonesome without community. but this forty years of sojourn in communal work has evolved into an inward journey of self recovery. whenever i enter community, it has to be out of this self discovery; whenever community enters my space, it will find me in this self recovery.

at sunset, i realize all the more that if i don't know myself how would it be possible to know someone else. 莊子 - Zhuangzi - admonishes: *he knows enough to recognize the faults of others; but knows not enough to recognize his own.* it is here that i find a restful place where God "makes me lie down in green pastures, beside quiet waters, that restores my soul in guided paths of righteousness." this restful quietude is not an end unto itself. it is a guided path toward self recovery, faults, fears, desires, dreads, and all.

i have never felt comfortable in my own skin, in solitude, in ministry, in community, in prayer. only by willful intentionality that i managed to get through a day in much of professional life. the notion of divine calling on my life kept me moving forward. even when i was plagued with self doubts, i have learned to doubt my doubts. people who care about me ask why i retire when there are opportunities for ministry. they assume that i have something to offer to community. i explain that many a week's end, i still open the word of God in some gathering somewhere, be it grudgingly and faintly enjoyable. i further explain that i have not retired from ministry but have retreated from people.

my retreat from full time ministry is due to a profound sense of infirmed lowliness. i step away from people primarily to seek a more holistic life. years ago, a useful tutorial in Enneagram provided a luminal revelation of my personality typology. since that self recovery, almost daily i am discovering my congenital sin of envy. the basis of all my decisions, struggles and insecurities come from this foundational sin of envy.

all my life i struggle with the pervasive feeling that something fundamental is missing in me. i always want something that others have. professionally, i envy those whose opportunities and giftedness have verged to bring them notoriety. personally, i envy those who are better off, physically, financially, intellectually and academically. this envy often has evolved into quiet resentment. i resent God in abject silence for his meager graces to me; i resent those who parade their gift wares in abject criticism. i especially resent those who, like me, are inferior and yet find success in fame and fortune.

that outward resentment has morphed into inward anguish. envy turns inward is a quiet feeling of despair, lowliness and loathing. painfully aware of my melancholy self-absorption, i long for comfort and joy, in community or in solitude. it was during the final months in California, after a horrific time of wallowing in self-doubt, i woke up one morning drenched in dread about the future. i mumbled an excuse to my family and drove west until i saw the water's edge of the Pacific ocean. while sitting under a palm tree, i was scraping the scabs of feeling sorry for myself. my bible and journal nested next to me on sifting sands. i looked hopelessly toward the infinity of the Pacific horizon.

it was a warm bright, breezy day but i was overcome by darkness. i opened my bible and wanted to read Luke, the gospel of Jesus i often come to when discouraged. but providence opened my bible to Matthew. from chapter 11, the word of Jesus spoke to me: "come to me, all you who are weary and burdened, and I will give you rest. take my yoke upon you and learn from me, for I am gentle and humble in heart, and you will find rest for your soul. for my yoke is easy and my burden is light."

i had read those words hundreds of time before, to the hearing of self and others. that day i heard it again and for the first time, i wanted Jesus' words to mean something. i read the passage over and over again hoping to conjure a divine epiphany. each time i finished i wanted God to break into my quiet desperation. nothing came. mildly upset, too tired to be agitated, i dismissed the silence as another disappointment with God. i closed my bible to scribble something in my journal. nothing came to me. so i closed my journal as well. i looked up to the ocean's infinite horizon again.

a moment lingered, as if time stopped, then as clear as the light of that beautiful day, i heard in English, "grace, righteous, winsome, rest. abide by them." at first, in amusement, i wondered where did the words come from. were they from God or from my hallucination. i thought i actually heard them audibly. at that moment, my cognition settled that what i heard was the voice of God speaking by my inner voice to my inner self. i resolved that they were from God and if there were doubts, i would doubt my doubts.

having settled that the words were a divine epiphany, i contemplated (share space with God) their meanings. immediately i opened Matthew passage, read it again and concluded that the spoken words were related to the written words. i scribbled "grace, righteous, winsome, rest" on a blank page in my journal. intuitively i touched the texture of the Matthew text along Jesus' words. then i strolled my fingers along the lines of the four words as i pronounced their sounds out loud. i closed my eyes to see the words. the moment lingered as i waited.

i did not know what to expected. a gradual calm draped over me - it was a joyous peaceableness that seemed to assuage my woes. i felt comforted. i looked out toward the ocean's edge again. suddenly, as if for the first time, i heard the crashing waves, smelled the salty air, tasted the savory mist. as if for the first time i had ever prayed, viscerally i blurted out in a whisper, "Lord. speak to my hearing." as clear as the sound of the crashing waves, that same voice whispered back, "abide by them and you will find rest." without hesitation i scribbled that phrase on the same page as the four words in my journal. i wanted to pray. i waited but no words came. at last, i folded my journal, got into my car and drove home as the sun set behind me.

day by day, i would come to that journal page with the four words to massage their meanings. weeks later, in solace of solitude i wrote in silence: in all things, with all people, live under God's grace. it's all you have; in all ways, with all people, do the right thing before God, it's all you can do; in all means, with all people, be winsome with God's grace-fullness, it's all you can be; in all circumstances, before all people, retreat to solitude to rest in God.

the four words have been translated into Chinese. a friend brushed them in calligraphy. for more than thirty years, the framed calligraphy hangs above my living room mantle as a consistent promise of rest from burdened weariness. in a daily, slow and certain light my darkness is illuminated. i am learning to take Jesus' light and easy yoke, to be gentle and humble in heart, and to find rest for your soul.

there is nothing better for this monk than to find rest at sunset. i take pleasure in reflecting the sunlight of the four words. self reflection germinates self understanding, an unhurried understanding blooms self recovery, and an ascendant recovery nurtures a deeper self awareness. every day's brightness filters into the sun room. here i read. twice a week, i browse the aisles of my local library and pull down volumes of infinite subjects that include biography, history, psychology, theology, philosophy. they complement my reading of the Bible. between books, i read about half a dozen periodicals. my readings become my companions who share daily nourishment with me. God is never more present when i am reading.

here i also write. i scribble my muses of ideas, insights, phrases, quotes and references. these muses are impetus for writings. my Enneagram shows that my personality typology has a creative bent. my self awareness is also self creative. there is great, plain pleasure in the writing process. there is little else more pleasurable than shaping introspective thoughts into concrete expressions. i lost myself and find myself in the very act of writing. God is never more close than when i am writing.

although enough people through the years have urged me to publish, toward the sunset years, i realize that i don't have the right stuff to write professionally.

16

whatever they find in my teaching, they almost gave me enough courage to pursue publication. but at sunset, there are three common senses that keeps me rational. first, after i read published authors like Bonhoeffer, Eugene Peterson, Karen Armstrong or Garry Wills, i fear that any prose less in excellence should stay unpublished. as i have felt for enough writers, including colleagues and acquaintances, i would be embarrassed to find a monograph of mine in the bookstore.

second, Emily Dickinson was a prolific poet, yet she did not publish during her life time. much of her work was published posthumously. i find that fascinating. her biographers agree that she felt her time and privacy were too precious. A recluse, she kept to herself and enjoyed what she wrote best. by no means i compare myself to this great poet. the good things we share are our jealous for privacy and our craving for time. third, there is really little i have to offer that others in a more excellent way have not given. besides, it is hard work to parade my written wares before publishers. it takes an enormous ego fed by ambition to take it happen. therefore, without this undue pressure from within or outside, i write daily and freely.

here i also brush paint. what i have learned from my Chinese brush teacher, i imitate in solitude. this also feeds my creative bent. like writing, painting also has an introspective stillness. in long stillness, i gaze outwardly at a painting, then copy its strokes within the limits of my skills. in long stillness, at times, i gaze inwardly of a visual image in my mind, then i imitate it with all the freedom of my imagination. twice weekly, i spend my mornings with my four friends - water, ink, brushes, paper. they enter my sad loneliness and transform it into solace of solitude. God is never more engrossed when i am painting.

the silence of reading, writing and painting is often filled with the delightful music of Bach. his cantatas for faith seasons' worship, solitary piano works and musical offerings permeate my room like morning sunlight. between the glory of Bach i also listen to Alan Jackson and George Strait's renditions of love and lost, blue mood and sky. their moody country twangs fill my soul as well.

noverim te, noverim me
that i may know me,
so that i may know you (God).
Augustine

at sun rise every morning, before the labor[‡] of reading, writing and painting, i work to know God. Augustine's light of knowing God through knowing self is a slow and progressive insight. for all these years since my conversion, i have gotten it wrong by seeking to know God without finding self. i have read the parable of lost many times but never reading it. Luke 15.17 reads plainly that before the prodigal son comes home to his waiting father, he first has to come to himself. it is in self discovery that we begin to experience God discovery. if i don't know my self, then i cannot know God, as God knows me. it is a grievous thing at first to embrace this disparaging notion of human mystery. but in time, the grievous becomes irresistibly self-affirming.

there is a irony in Augustine's light - when i was younger in faith, i actually felt closer to God. that felt closeness came from immaturity, inexperience and self unawareness. i entered prayers with a certain confidence that was oblivious to self and God. my fealty is defined more by a false confidence of self as well as a false assurance of knowing God. then the

---

[‡] *these are two of three ideas - work, labor and action - of Hannah Arendt's fundamental meanings of being human in "The Human Condition."*

disappointments of God's hiddenness in my prayer life began to hedge me in. there were long spells when i could not pray because prayers felt like speaking into the air. during those long years of ministry years, i didn't pray in solitude but prayed with all the aplomb of professionalism with my congregants in community.

at sunset, i recover prayers again. my prayers are always out of and in silence. my imposed silence makes good communion with God. at sunrise, i commune with God in my adapted version *lectio divina.* during communion, i sit in silence and journal into a blank page. my scribbles fill no more and no less than a single page. this reflection is probably the most transparent exercise of communion with God. my thoughts are unvarnished, unharnessed and roam without propriety.

then an assigned passage of the Bible is read. the regiment usually following the text of a Biblical book. i may read the passage many times with many translations that includes the Chinese. while the passage is open to me, i rummage other authors to find light to illuminate my reading. while i read and wait, their insights become divine light on the sacred page. in this work of silence, the sacred text informs my mind, reforms my heart and forms my soul.

with the passage still opens before me, i retreat to the other side of my journal page. in contemplation i respond to God in written prayers. the words of the assigned text guide my rambling thoughts. the text is more a dividing lane marking than a guarding rail. i empty my aching heart and troubled soul in earnest. this exercise is equally transparent. my words are pre-meditated but unhindered. just as i am full from my readings, i empty myself in prayer. after prayer i close my Bible and journal. the remains of the day is my day in contemplation - sharing space with God. whether in solitude or in community, my communion with God is not always pretty or pious; it may be ugly and unregenerate, but always in contemplation.

自然
the natural true self
老子 Lao-Tze

this solace of solitude has a span for loneliness. Henri Nouwen writes about transforming loneliness into solitude. even at the sunset years of my pilgrimage toward faith, i have not mastered the mastery of solitude. whether with people or with self, my loneliness is ubiquitous. at sunset, while in contemplation, i realize all the more the saving grace of God. as loneliness slowly morphs into solitude, i am never more my true self. when alone, the natural true self Lao-Tze refers to is my real presence with self.

i realize that i am only at the threshold of self discovery; i am only beginning to cultivate a truer self. many years of perpetrating a false self is difficult to break. i recall that during those years in community, i was never comfortable in my own skin. and living a false self seemed the only way to cope. it took a great source of intentionality to get through a day in falsehood. i played a role, acted out a purpose, fulfilled a task. but now in sunset, perhaps for the first time, i experience a truer self, a natural truer self.

this naturalism is freeing; but there is danger here. when i am alone. my newfound freedom can easily morph into reckless disregard for sobriety. my thoughts race wild in the muddy sludge of depravity. my thoughts easily submerge under unwholesome images. what Paul calls the works of the flesh:

fornication, impurity, licentiousness, idolatry, sorcery, enmities, strife, jealously, anger, quarrels, dissensions, factions, envy, drunkenness, carousing. my preoccupation transgresses this endless listing of the work of the flesh.

Lao-Tze believes that humanity is naturally good. his naturalism does not recognize original sin. at sunset this monk recognizes acutely how pervasive is sinful human nature. to experience a true presence is also to cope with the dark side of my true nature. *"You are a wild flower that never bloomed,"* a friend said to me in passing. little did he realize that his inadvertent observation defines my natural true self. his phrasing of who he thought i am emerged out of a twenty-year friendship. he had engaged with me in every role i played everywhere - as pastor, as son, as father, as husband, as spouse and as his friend with others.

this comment over a drink was a profundity beyond our sensibility. little did we realize that this iconic image of a wild flower that never bloomed captures the essence of my truer self. this wasn't the beginning of my self-recovery, but it certainly lay out the foundational idea for self discovery. at sunset, it becomes clear that in the three epochs of my journey - from adolescence to professional work, from church to denominational works, from seminary professor to a monk in retreat at sunset - i have always been a wild flower that never truly bloomed.

i lived for others; i play-acted for others. in the many guises of professional work and in the many performances of public holiness, i have perpetrated a quiet image. this guarded image dictated almost everything i did and said in community. with very few exceptions, i was never in real presence. living a false self for so long, even in private, sometimes i forgot who i was and ignored what i had become. too many times, i actually believed that i was that person whom i was perpetrated.

this gift of insight from a friend provides light to see who i am and what i need to be. those four words - grace, righteous, winsome, rest - from God under the palm tree one summer day many years ago stay true during sunset at winter. the words are light unto my inward path toward self recovery. this thought of a wild flower that never bloomed has been my unfinished singular muse. my contemplative life at sunset is to bloom a wild flower into a graceful, righteous, winsome and restful bouquet:

an underwhelmed ego. when i was a little bud in my mother's womb, a curse by evil relatives scarred me for life. they burned incents to heaven that i would born a girl. my mother was anxious that i would be a boy. when i was a month old, she sent a naked, full frontal photograph of me to my father. she wanted to reassure him that i had a penis and the curse did not prevail. when i was eight, my mother and i came to America. we were here but a few weeks when my parents took me to pay respect to a village elder. this laundry man was senselessly cruel. he glanced my way and predicted that i would never amount to anything, that i would work by the swear of my brow for the rest of my life to make a living. my parents were deeply insulted. on our way home, my mother called me by my full Chinese name and sternly exhorted me to prove him wrong.

since that traumatic episode, the damaging scars on my soul have done their work. the possibility that i was fated to fail in life's endeavors has haunted me to this day. i suppose every decision i have made for work, every endeavor i have pursued at work was motivated by this subconscious fear of failure. there are people who consider me a success; they behold my resume with affirmation. regardless of my apparent success, i have never felt that i have proved the elder wrong. the pervasive feeling that i am never good enough to prove him wrong lingers to this day.

like the self-deprecating comedian, Rodney Dangerfield, i have never escaped the notion that "I don't get no respect!" accolades come and go, but a single criticism lingers forever. while i have dismissed praises as polite lies, yet secretly i crave for respect. in quiet desperation, i have sought respect from congregants at church and colleagues at work. from faculty to students at school, from family and friends. i die a thousand deaths longing for their affirmation. too many times i have even begged my wife to approve me even if she has to pretend. but she does not acknowledge my need. it seems i can never receive enough respect.

craving for demonstrative respect is still a struggle. but i am learning to cope with slices of negativity, inadvertent insults and intentional impudence. the desert fathers and mothers warn that the road to humility is humiliation. i have never prayed for humility, knowing that i will have more than my share of humiliation. at sunset, my underwhelmed ego is still a crippling pathology. but at the end of my day, as God's day begin for me,[§] i feel better than i have ever before. a good portion of self recovery is self acceptance as i am learning to live in gracefulness, righteousness, winsomeness and restfulness.

an angry spirit. the latent anger has always been there since my youth. it comes with regularity that has often

---

[§] *in Genesis creation narrative, God marks his days as evening and morning. the day begins at sunset.*

metamorphosed into melancholy. some days are worst than others. it drags me into a black hole of self loathing. to this day, i have never felt comfortable with who i am and what i have become. i have always felt that there is much to disdain.

my anger has also been an anguish toward the outside world. often it has metamorphosed into anxiety. this proverbial village has always felt like a disparaging place for work, labor and act, Arendt's three human endeavors. it is irreparably broken - machines break down, cars slam into each other, planes fall from the sky. it is socially chaotic. people make mistakes, misunderstand and misplace things. the social currency of loyalty, conversations, sensibility and quietude is counterfeited. it is a dangerous arena. so many bad things happen. millions become homeless from a relentless flood. a ferocious hurricane roars in and destroys families. i have never felt safe here.

my anger has also been plainly a profound disappointment with God. dancing with my emotive responses to reality, the facts of life are stubborn for resentment. my cognitive knowledge has stepped on my toe of faith too many times. i have never been able to reconcile the goodness of God and an irreparably broken world. and yet at sunset, day by day, my angry soul is tutored by the graceful, righteous, winsome and restful quietude of simple faith. daily in contemplation, my heart confesses that if i understand God than the God of my understanding would not be God. i am learning to doubt my doubts. then, it is only in doubting my doubts that i realize that this world, the narrow space of my own doing, can be a better place, when i purpose to live those four words. and just as quietly, gratitude enters in.

a tortured soul. the words *tortured* and *damaged* are different but similar in their meanings. a damaged soul suffers an impairment that renders it incapable of wholesome responses to the demands of social intercourse. a tortured soul suffers pains that robs it joy in the good things, albeit few, the world has to offer. the damages and torture are existentially connected to my many years of incapacity to engage community and enjoy people.

it has often seemed that life has passed me by in the dark of night. so many dreams have been day-mares; so many opportunities have been missed. since that first disappointment with God in my first year of ministry, it seemed life and life work have been a continuity of disappointment. there have been many a day when i wake up full of dread; there have been many a day when my work seemed to naught. many a day, self- contempt bordered on self-hatred.

now at sunset, i realize for whatever the albatross, there is little i can do in community or in solitude, except to weep in brokenness. over the years, i have wept in brokenness on three separate occasions. in effect, they become analogous to my brokenness.

the first time was at a denominational annual meeting. after evening worship, we were invited to pray with another. a good friend and colleague was sitting next to me, so we turned to pray together. after his prayers, i prayed. overwhelmed by a profound sense of unworthiness before God, suddenly i began to sob uncontrollably. my friend awkwardly put his hand on my shoulder and waited in quietude. my weeping lingered for a while until finally i collected myself. at another time and another place with another, i would have been humiliated. but not this time, for my friend was graceful with a quietude.

the second time i wept was in the thick of a church plant in the middle of Manhattan. my congregants were a difficult bunch. they bickered, complained, questioned, resisted at every turn. they agonizingly worn me out. during a church board meeting, in mid sentence, suddenly i sobbed uncontrollably. overwhelmed by a profound sense of incompetence, i plainly did not want to do pastoral work anymore. my inexperienced young leaders did not know what to do. but they had enough presence of mine to wait in silence. when i finally subsided, they offered a sabbatical. in time, i left church work as i had left my church board that night and went home in the dark of night.

the third time i embraced my daughter to say good bye before she drove home to Boston. the night before we had gotten into a taut argument about my concern for her. like so many conversations with so many others, this one was also laced with miscommunication and misunderstanding. holding her tightly, i whispered, i love her, and she said, i loved you too. suddenly i sobbed uncontrollably. it was a long embrace as we held each other tightly. finally i let her go. as i watched her car drove away, i wept again. intermittently i wept for two days, overwhelmed by a sense of inadequacy as her father and conquered by a sense of utter helplessness to bring her happiness. i was also overcome by a profound regret that i have made a mess of every person i have touched in my family, including my wife, my four children and my sister.

at sunset, i cry easily and often. a poignant scene in a movie, a tragedy of an acquaintance or a stranger, a birthday celebration for my grandchildren, a disappointment with someone, a proud moment with my adult children, a thoughtful gift - i weep, recognizing my unworthiness with God, my incompetence with people and my inadequacy with family. in this winter of my discontent, there is little else but to embrace the four words, day by day, from moment to moment.

a contrarian mind. my faith has been brought up in the disinfectant soil of American evangelicalism. but as an adult believer, i have never found an emotive connection with its confessions. American evangelicalism is immediately insecure, arrogant, dogmatic and shallow. its theological scholarship is dishonest, pretentious, narrow and timorous. at once, it is fatuous in engagement between faith and practice. as one observer noted, evangelicals are moralistic, therapeutic and practicing deists.

our confessional dogma does not translate well in daily life. we are moralistic in our understanding of spirituality. all we seem to have are the Lord's prayer and the ten commandments. our faith in Jesus is therapeutic. we are desirous more than anything that our Lord would make us feel good, look good and make good. as deists we want God to be far away, until when we are in trouble and need our petitioned prayers answered.

too many studies have shown that evangelicalism is waning in the public square. our presence in society is innocuous. in fact, these same studies show that Christians live not too differently from the greater society, in convictions, values and beliefs. my ministry in a span of forty years has exposed the three great contexts of Christianity - the local church, the denominational office and the seminary. having been in these three places, emptied of energy. i struggle to find either strength or courage to participate in their work.

i have always recognized that the church is the only game in town. if i didn't play faith here, there is no other arena to play religion. when i retreated from full time ministry, it was a departure from evangelicalism but not from church. with guarded sobriety, i held my peace and kept this sentiment to my self.

at sunset, without a home church for ministry, my wife and i sought a local church as our faith's home. much of what we experienced in the past years there is wanting, its pastoral leadership, ministry of the word, communal life, liturgy and worship. no one knows my angst for the church except for a friend of my wife. but she doesn't empathize nor understand. i am undeniably, excruciatingly, irreversibly and irreparably a reluctant adherent of the church as my faith community.

i don't seek opportunities to do ministry but i don't resist opportunities for pastoral work. many week's days, i meet with young and old pastors to talk about them and their work. many week's ends are filled with pastoral work. i speak into the air my hermeneutics of God's word. i engage groups of couples and individuals with God's word as we seek to cut a path of human living. at all times, i take quiet pleasure in cutting against the soft grains of traditional Evangelicalism. but at the remains of the day, i enter these communities deeply aware of my four words. they shape the ways i practice hospitality with those who enter my space.

a bohemian heart. in my heart of hearts, i long for a bohemian life, a life that roams wildly. there has always been a propensity to riot in social conventions. my lusts for life are those strong promiscuous urges, urges that cut across traditional morality. in a fleeting moment of unusual transparency, a fellow pastor confessed among colleagues that if he was not a pastor, he would play the field with women; if not a Christian he would sleep round. his strong polygamous tendencies were hand tied only by the thin rope of ecclesiastical conventionality. "what would people in church think if they knew," he asked out loud.

no one offered a response, as he took a glance at his attractive secretary with a wink. pretending that i was not aware of his intimation, i looked him blankly. but little did anyone realize that his confessional sentiments were not far from my quiet desperation. since my college years, multiple lusty demons have been lurking in the dark basement of my soul. when the sun sets into night, when the sky is dark, when my body aches in loneliness, when my body is far from the maddening crowds, these demons hiss poisonous thoughts and gesture lewd acts into my imagination. through the years i have played the role and acted the part of a cleric with trembling hypocrisy. some years were more apropos than others. often without actual working, i have parroted Augustine's disingenuous petition, *fac me bonum deus meus, sed noli modo.* faithfulness in work and wedlock was not always dispersed willfully, nor procurably. even at sunset, indulgent struggles are ever present, if not more so.

but it is more of mind than of body. if this is kind of victory, it is a small one. my self-suppression hangs on two reasons. for those earlier years it was the propriety of professional ministry. the choke of my cleric collar strangled much wilding impulse out of the body. it had kept the demons in the subterranean of my homesick blues. at sunset, the choke of the cleric collar is loosened. but there is a lockbox in which much of these wayward memories are kept and put away. and, of course, the four words remain; they hedge me in and assuage my demonic angst. but i remain a wild flower that never bloomed. as long as there is warmth in this body, i am excruciatingly, painfully, cripplingly, incurably and miserably trapped in an aesthetic mortification. in another opportunity, another dirt field, and another grassy meadow, i would go wilding far away from the conventional.

a non-conformist. years ago, a great tool of self discovery exposes my truer self. since that discovery i have recovered my self in incremental awareness. it proves to be entirely liberating. the Enneagram uncovers this individual wild flower. in my best moments, i am creative, expressive, inspiring, passionate, sensitive and sensible. in my worst moments, i am angry, depressed, alienating, fatigued, morbid, despairing and disparaging.

my great sin is envious of others; my greater desire is to find my true self; my greatest fear is lack of real significance. throughout my professional years i have looked at other professionals with notoriety with private envy. how i have wished to swap lives with them. i have sought more earnest in caging this envious monster than those lustful demons. perhaps that is why i have been more empowered in killing the sin of envy than the demons of lust. since my middle years, i have vowed never to seek a position, promotion or recognition.

when my seminary offered a directorship to run an academic program, i said no; when a parachurch organization offered to honor my life work in ministry, i declined. but the monster of envy is a stubborn beast of burden. it is only at sunset in self recovery that i am slowly coming to term with my potentials and limitations. in true, i regret that i have only been at the outer perimeter of recognition. i often joke with people that i am like a small town beauty queen. they, the town folks, encourage me to compete in bigger venues for greater fame. i smile knowing i don't have the right beauty nor the right stuff.

many times i blame God. for God has not found it wise to grant me the giftedness or the episodic moment to step on main stage. such is my lot. at sunset, non-conformity affirms my natural truer self. when i stepped over sixty years of age, a tattoo of a black sheep making out with a shepherd's crook on my forearm celebrated the rite of passage. making out with a black sheep behind the altar of my vocation has been a love-hate endeavor.

at sunset, while living in some resemblance of serenity, my great comfort is that i have been different from the ordinary. whatever accomplishments or failures, what realized endeavors or broken dreams, what came my ways or missed my stop, i take comfort in that i have not conformed to the prosaic. with gracefulness, righteousness, winsomeness and restfulness, i want others to enter or leave my contemplation appreciative of the differences i have made.

an aesthetic sensory. i am at my best, most comfortably, and more joyfully when i am in aesthetic creativity. when i am scribing a sermon, brushing a plum blossom, snapping a photograph, it is well with my soul. something as banal as setting the table for dinner with guests becomes most satisfying when there is aesthetic symmetry with the dinner wares. it is equally gratifying when i am designing a slide presentation to enhance a lecture. it is also effectuating to gaze upon Vincent's Wheat Fields, watch Hitchcock's Rear Window or listen to Haddon Roberson's phrasings.

once the creative process is done, there is nothing to look forward to. when i lost my voice after forty years of taxing my vocal cords in public speaking, the speech therapist taught me to relearn how to speak again. little did she realize how much public speaking taxed my soul. the irony is that much of my professional work has been public speaking. and yet the aesthetic journey from formless thoughts to a formed monologue ends when i stand in community to speak. the joy of the aesthetic work digresses into drudgery of labor.

in fact, whatever medium, after the creative process is done, i have no desire to display it. actually this is not entirely true. C. S. Lewis is very agreeable when he writes that the praise of an object completes our joy of it. that is, the joy of my scribed sermon or brushed plum blossom is incomplete until i offer it to the praise of others. when others enjoy my voice performance or my painting, it does complete the pleasure of my creative process.

but i have never been good at professing my wares in public. you would think that my longing for significance would propel me to publish my writings or exhibit my paintings. i blame it on my underwhelming ego. my longing for significance is nullified by my fear for insignificance. at sunset, i realize that i am the happiest when i am with my readings, writings and paintings. and i am the unhappiest when when i am with my unshared readings, unpublished writings and un-displayed paintings. at the end of the day, at sunset, there but the gracefulness, righteousness, winsomeness and restfulness go i.

多言數窮　不如守中
more words are poor; prefer hold fast to center
孔子 Kung Tze

as i recently offered to a friend my decision to retreat from community, sitting at sunset, i cannot be in a better place. in solace of solitude, i read, write, paint and pray. out of solace into community, i speak into the air those things that are burning my heart. whether in solitude or in community, i am care-full to use fewer words. for indeed, the sage is wise beyond us. in solitude, there have been days when i utter almost no sounds. in community i discipline to make fewer sounds as possible. for indeed more words are poor. holding fast to my center in silence is a truer presence.

after twenty and more years, i have gotten accustomed to this country house at sunset. who would have predicted that i would settle here for good until the sun sets upon me? at their sunset years, Kung Tze and Lao Tze also retreated to their solitude. they give me courage to retreat from community. i suppose all who love wisdom see the world in a stranger light. where ever we have been, at sunset, we have to retreat to self.

the clarity of self-recovery comes from an imagination in self awareness. the wild flower that never bloomed image is full of self contradiction, as the self is incongruous within. but what human ontology is neat and orderly. human existence is a mystery, a human life a plight of conundrum. even in chaotic inner realities, one can still find stream of consciousness toward congruity of self awareness.

the four words from God continue to nurture my interior, in solitude and in community. they continue to cut a path toward self recovery, in gracefulness, righteousness, winsomeness and restfulness. through the middle years, resting on those assuring words, i have refined five daily *less and more* contemplatives while in solitude:

silence, speak less, ponder more
grace is lived and enjoyed in cleansing silence. when i imagine grace, i envision the iconic image in Mary, the mother of Jesus. she is a woman of few words. when the shepherds come to behold the infant Christ, the uproar of their excitement filled their stay with noises. this is written of her: but Mary treasured up all these things, pondering them in her heart. enough written, and there is something profoundly grace-full about silence. those moments and days when in silence i ponder all good thoughts of God's grace-filled presence. it is in silence where the enjoyment God's presence is more appreciated. likewise, often it is out of silence where the fullness of the creative process is more realized. i am never more aware of God's presence than in silence.

frugality, spend less, enjoy more
anxiety is pervasive in this post-modern world. psychology explains it as an anxiety of abundance. we are anxious because we have too much. never mind others. plainly, i have too much - clothes, gadgetries, collectables, plants, even books. my son alerts this propensity to his father. to want more is an addiction that diminishes the pleasure of what we already have. at sunset, i realize more acutely that the feel-good moment of owning something new fades haphazardly.

the more i buy, the less i enjoy; the more i own, the less i find meaningful. there is gracefulness in simplicity, in owning fewer things. a good portion of grace is the blessedness of owning nothing; a good portion of righteousness is to refrain from accumulating more; a good portion of rest is to enjoy what i already have. in post- modern materialism, it is excruciatingly difficult to want less. to kill this urge of wanting more and more, during certain seasons of faith, i impose moratoriums on spending. i plainly refuses to buy anymore new things.

moderation, eat less, live more
in my middle years, my middle becomes flabby. i enjoy food. there is nothing more grand than to enjoy good food in good fellowship with good friends. in truth, i definitely look better with clothes than without. at sunset, even flattering clothes cannot flatter this slow metabolism of an aging body. less consumption of food is more than for good looks. it is also a pursuit of self control that leads to spiritual reformation. i dare write that self control is probably the last conquest of spirituality. during the course of my weeks, in solitude or in community, i live and die by the seven "s" food rules: when in solitude, a small breakfast in mid morning with a *single* full meal in mid afternoon, i *snack* not; when in community, i do not have a *second serving*, eat something *sweet*, i refrain from *social eating*. at all times i avoid *starchy food*. with those days that begin with a *"s"* -Saturday and Sunday - i enjoy the common three meals, in moderation.

reading, watch less, reflect more
in sadness and loneliness, the nights own me. easily the senseless thing to do is to fill the void with the mind-numbing television glare. the wave and ebb of loneliness plays a critical role. those in the room also play a part. when loneliness is not yet solitude, the

insane urge to click on the television. it is so effortless, it is almost mindless. the irony is that with 200 channels and more, there is nothing to watch. still I watch. a better portion of grace is to watch less. so i regiment my viewing time. only a limited number of shows are allotted weekly. for every new watch, i have to reduce an old watch. to fill the void, i read reflectively.   good reads - books, magazines, newspapers, electronic print media - are everywhere. every sitting space at sunset has offerings of reading that nourishes a restful mind, soul and heart. i read daily at long duration.

hospitality, seek less community, welcome all
at sunset, there is nothing more valued than less community and more solitude. again, because of weakness of mind and weariness of soul that I retreat from community. my soul's consensus is to guard solitude daily. but when grace and rest are experienced in solitude, there is the work of winsomeness and righteousness in community. solitude is both a departure from and a preparation for community. it would be graceless to seek solitude at the expense of community. although community is hard work, it is also grace-full. hospitality means plainly that my presence becomes the presence of God. in God's presence i welcome anyone who desires communion with me. i enter community always with the warmth of hospitality.

during the early years of pastoral work, i attended to Tozer's tutelage on vows making for ministry. vows are promises i made to myself when engaging in church work. they are an iron railing from a precipice; a trespass sign on someone's property, lane markers on a highway, a rock cleft in a howling storm. these vows have guided and guarded me since. subsequently, as i sought to develop a philosophy for ministry, in time, they become a philosophy for community.

two sets of *always* and *never* were etched on the interior walls of my mind - actually they are two pieces of paper on my desk. many trials and errors, comfort and joy, courage and fear have gone into their final form. as the *less and more* contemplatives are in solitude, these *always and never* vows act their part in community. in every imperfect community, these resolves have protected me from bad people and vindicated me for good intentions.

never defend myself
in all circumstances, as imperfect that we all are, people of disparaging motives have complained, made accusations, gossiped, spoken wrong about me. all these years, as far as i can tell, i have never defended myself in private or in public. when others in crises of conflict made accusations against me, on three episodic occasions in 1986, 1993, 2002, i purposed to keep silent. if the accusations are true, i seek God's mercies. if the accusations are false, i seek God's justice. never have i sought self defense. Tozer writes that God is a more potent to defend us than our poorer power. this resolve has not always been pleasant to work out. but among many other regrets, i have never regretted for not speaking up in my own defense.

never give counsel unless asked
when i engage in conversation with others, seldom do i speak first. if i do, it is most likely in a form of a question. if they come for counsel, my resolve is still the same. seldom do i offer advise. even when asked, i intentionally ignore the request. most people ask something not to hear my voice but to hear their own. an anxious mother, whose son is contemplating full time ministry, cornered me at a church function to seek

my "counsel on what she should do." i listened as she talked for twenty minutes describing her perspectives. she asked me several about this or that but never stopped to listen. i kept my peace. finally, she thanked me and walked away with her husband. i could only smirk – who am i to give counsel to this talkative woman? i can hardly take care of my own woes.

never own anything
once a big shot pastor was introduced to me by his associate. but he had no time for me and ignored me after we exchanged greetings. i watched his back as he walked away. once a friend reminded me three times in one day that i owed him an additional two euros for our shared car service from the airport. i never travel with him again. i don't like people who are parsimonious with their time or money. they upset the graces of our meager living. on the other hand, generous people are gracious. they enrich the graces of life. to be winsome, i must be generous; to be graceful i need to be generous. to be generous i cannot hoard what i own. certain things are easier to give away. books are not one of them. i have freely shared my home, car, gadgets and money with others. but not my books. mainly because people don't treat them with respect. at sunset, i am working on loosening my grip on my books.

never seek recognition or position
in all my professional work, i have never sought recognition or a position. my impoverished soul does not always agree with this resolve. a promotion at an apropos moment is an affirming thing for a position conducted well. a plaque on an office wall is a sure sign that those i serve appreciate me. some accolade every now and then is tasty morsel for a hungry soul. but my cognition disagrees. all these years i have never sought a position, promotion or advancement. in fact, i have

declined several offers through the years. the few that i have accepted are usually for more practical reasons. when i applied for an associate professorship at the seminary it was for a $6,000 pay raise, not for the promotion. once a para-church organization wanted to honor me for my life work. i probably insulted the organizer when i laughed out loud, "who? me? what life work are you talking about!"

never take self seriously
sarcasm, irony and cynicism roamed unbound in many of my encounters during those early years. how else could i cope with community. in later years, i have learned to rein in these defenses with better control. i deploy them to poke fun at myself as well as at others. during my first class of every semester, i introduce myself with these words: "make sure you are in the right class. you pay good money for this class. you need to know that i really don't know anything. and what i know is useless to you . . . but its your money." although i speak in earnest, most students don't believe me. nevertheless, self deprecation is genuine because i don't take self seriously. making fun of my self has always come easily. i certainly take what i do seriously, even when a clown is doing it.

never second guess others
being human that we all are, it is impossible to know what another is thinking or feeling when s/he is speaking. the one speaking may be strong or meek, wise or stupid, pious or impious, pleasant or onerous. his subconscious is so deep, i suspect he doesn't know what is going on in there. her pathology is so convoluted she has no clue about herself. it is no use trying to know people. whether at a dinner table with others or one on one in my office, i don't surmise nor do i say much. i try to listen in earnest for silence is probably the most graceful way to invite God to work

his grace into the conversation. otherwise, the strangeness of others is burdensome to me. more importantly, when i refrain from second guess others, i am stronger to resist from talking down to, judging, or condemning them.

never forget who are my enemies
Jesus says i have to love my enemies, but i don't have to like them. and i certainly don't have to hang out with them. when possible, i avoid them as if they have a contagious disease. i can never forget what they did and why they did it. but what does it mean to love them. i settle for this - if they are in need, and i can meet that need, and if they ask me to meet that need, i will reach out to them with all the determination of cognitive love.

to be sure, i hope the righteousness of God will prevail. i do whatever is true, noble, right, pure, lovely, is admirable and praiseworthy. this has not always be easy. but doing what is righteous has never been easy for me. my wife in so many words says many times that i don't have a good heart. even with a bad heart, i can find it in me to forgive in time. but regardless of time, i can never forget my enemies.

always be hospitable to all
as mentioned earlier, my tattered soul is simply too flimsy to portage the heaviness of community. i fail others; others fail me. even in weakness, in long moments of solace, i am still committed to community by the warmth of hospitality. although i don't seek it, i make it my intention to welcome those who seek communion with me. Bonheoffer is wise with this: we must be ready to allow ourselves to be interrupted by God. God will be constantly crossing our paths, canceling our plans with people. . .

in fact, much interruption to my solitude is others' need for hospitality. some encounters are harder to welcome than other. many are draining; few are nourishing. and yet, at the remains of the day, every encounter is an appointment of God. hanging in my solitary room are these words in Chinese calligraphy - 尋 不 而 迎 - *seek not, always welcome.* while in solace of solitude, they constantly remain me that every interruption is an opportunity for community.

always be generous with all things
also mentioned before, generosity is a good portion of being winsome. winsomeness to all is to be generous with all. of course, it is easier to be generous with some things for some people. space and possessions are easily shared; time and books are more difficult. yet Jesus' saying that it is indeed more blessed to give than to receive proves to be true every time. the older i get, the longer at sunset, the more i realize how pleasurable it is to share what i am and have with others. mostly, being generous completes what i have become.

always find better light in all encounters
this endeavor is more attitude than action. both my theology and experience verify that we humans are broken beyond repair. given my pessimistic bent, it is so natural to think the worst of people. most don't do well with a good front. a veneer at best. they give themselves away at their first sound in conversation. yet i realize that how i see others is more a reflection of my deficiency than their depravity. by an act of the will, if i have to assume something about them, i seek to find others in a better light. intentionally naive, i act toward them as if they are better people than they actually are. with great sobriety and sensibility, i engage with them *as if there is encouragement in Christ, comfort from his shared love and with enough affection and sympathy.*

always listen before speaking
"be kind, for everyone you meet is fighting a great battle," so says Philo, a Greek philosopher of Jewish ancestry. indeed, if kindness is the best response, it is best offered with listening. here is the thing - most people are more eager to hear their own voice than mine. the righteous thing to do, the winsome thing to do is to be quick to listen, and slow to speak. Job lamented that if his chatty friends had kept quiet, he would gladly mistake their silence for wisdom, Job 13.5. whatever i am doing with others, i would want all to walk away feeling that i have been wise.

always leave all spaces a better place
it was also Job who recognized this, "I could strengthen you with my mouth; the solace of my lips would assuage your pains." Job 16.6. if there is a human soul who qualifies to know pain, it would be Job. i learn daily that whenever i enter conversations, if i must speak, the solace of my lips must assuage the pains in others. there is no other way to practice winsomeness. now the solace of words can mean different scenarios to different people. it can be words of encouragement, hope or empathy. years ago a friend admits that he would bend his theology momentarily to give courage to another. how can i disagree. it can be a brief prayer. i seldom promise to pray for someone, but i would pray with that person at once. most of the times, it is a quiet serenity of utter silence. my body language is all i can say.

always find joy in all circumstances.
what Helen Hayes said about charm, i say about joy. without joy, nothing matters, with joy, nothing else matters. where ever i am, i have to live with my self. even if i forget where i am, at the remains of the day, i will find my way back to my self. with self, joy is the hardest virtue to possess. it does not flow easily into

44

my stream of consciousness. i have to steal joy in whatever circumstances. sometimes, i consider it a joy to enjoy a cup of good coffee with hazelnut and cream. it is consolation enough to brave through a miserable encounter. another time, an unexpected word of encouragement inadvertently given is affirmation enough to feel good about myself in a discouraging circumstance. how else can i find rest for my soul in community.

this is my center, a center based on a profound self awareness of overwhelming unworthiness, of incredulous incompetence, and of grievous repentance. it is also a center of self acceptance, and of God acceptance. there is nothing more i can do to find grace, righteousness, winsomeness and rest. at sunset i am never more comfortable with my self, with God and with others. these words from Isaiah 11.10 quoting out of context fits well in my context: . . . *and His resting place will be glorious* . . .

meanwhile, i remain - *in qui solus est cum solus* - the one who is alone with alone.